NICE WORK, FRANKLIN!

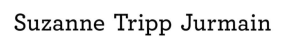

Suzanne Tripp Jurmain

illustrations by

Larry Day

DIAL BOOKS FOR YOUNG READERS

DIAL BOOKS FOR YOUNG READERS · Penguin Young Readers Group
An imprint of Penguin Random House, LLC, 375 Hudson Street, New York, NY 10014

Library of Congress Cataloging-in-Publication Data · Jurmain, Suzanne. · Nice work, Franklin! / by Suzanne Tripp Jurmain; illustrated by Larry Day. · pages cm · ISBN 978-0-8037-3800-3 (hardcover)
1. Roosevelt, Franklin D. (Franklin Delano), 1882–1945—Juvenile literature. 2. Presidents—United States—Biography—Juvenile literature. I. Day, Larry, date, illustrator. II. Title. · E807.J87 2016   973.917092—dc23   [B]   2014048073
II. Title.   PZ7.H1295Bhm 2014   [E]—dc23   2013027092

Printed in China
1 3 5 7 9 10 8 6 4 2
Designed by Jason Henry · Text set in Archer
The artwork for this book was created with Wolff pencil and watercolor with gouache.

Special thanks to Jim Mills, archivist, St. Thomas's Parish, Washington, DC,
and Robert Clark, Acting Director, Franklin D. Roosevelt Presidential Library and Museum.

★ ★ ★ ★   SELECTED BIBLIOGRAPHY   ★ ★ ★ ★

Cohen, Adam. *Nothing to Fear: FDR's Inner Circle and the Hundred Days that Created Modern America.* Penguin: New York, 2009.

Flynn, Katherine A., and Richard Polese. *The New Deal: A 75th Anniversary Celebration.* Gibbs Smith: Salt Lake City, Utah, 2008.

Gunther, John. *Roosevelt in Retrospect: A Profile in History.* Harper: New York, 1950.

Kennedy, David M. *Freedom from Fear: The American People in Depression and War 1929–1945.* Oxford University Press: New York, 1999.

Levine, Lawrence W., and Cornelia R. Levine. *The People and the President: America's Conversation with FDR.* Beacon Press: Boston, 2002.

Miller, Nathan. *FDR: An Intimate History. Madison Books:* Lanham, MD, 1983.

Moley, Raymond. *After Seven Years.* Harper: New York, 1939.

Perkins, Frances. *The Roosevelt I Knew.* Viking: New York, 1946.

Roosevelt, Curtis. *Too Close to the Sun: Growing Up in the Shadow of My Grandparents, Franklin and Eleanor.* Perseus Book Group: Philadelphia, PA, 2008.

Roosevelt, Eleanor. *The Autobiography of Eleanor Roosevelt.* Da Capo Press: New York, 1992.

Roosevelt, Elliott, and James Brough. *An Untold Story: The Roosevelts of Hyde Park.* Putnam: New York, 1973.

Roosevelt, Franklin D. *Fireside Chat,* March 12, 1933.
www.presidency.ucsb.edu/ws/index.php?pid=14540.

_____. *First Inaugural Address,* March 4, 1933. www.bartleby.com/124/pres49.html.

_____. *Second Inaugural Address,* January 20, 1937, www.bartleby.com/124/pres50.html.

Smith, Jean Edward. *FDR.* Random House: New York, 2007.

Taylor, Nick. *American-Made: The Enduring Legacy of the WPA: When FDR Put the Nation to Work.* Bantam Dell: New York, 2008.

Ward, Geoffrey C. *A First-Class Temperament: The Emergence of Franklin Roosevelt.* Harper & Row: New York, 1989.

_____. *Before the Trumpet: Young Franklin Roosevelt 1882–1905.* Ward Press: kindle edition. 2013.

Webber, Michael J. "Election of 1936" in the *Encyclopedia of the Great Depression,* Macmillan Reference USA, pp. 285–290. Gale Cenage Learning, 2009.

http://media-server.amazon.com

For Steve Meltzer—who makes good things happen
−S.T.J.

For Miriam—for her visual insight and intuition
−L.D.

★

Do Presidents Have Challenges?

You'd better believe it.

Some of those challenges are personal and some are national. President William Howard Taft had a personal challenge. He always had to worry about gaining too much weight. President George Washington had a national challenge. He had to figure out how to start up a brand-new country. And some presidents get a double whammy.

Abraham Lincoln had to end slavery, fight the Civil War, and listen to people say mean things about him. Still, Lincoln was up to the challenge. He won the war. He freed the slaves. And when folks said he was "ugly" and "two-faced," Lincoln shot back: "If I am two-faced, would I wear the face that I have now?" President Theodore Roosevelt didn't do as well. He managed to clean up the nation's food supply, start national parks, and make big US businesses behave. But when someone said that his daughter Alice was doing wild and crazy things, like keeping a real live snake up her sleeve, Roosevelt threw up his hands. He said, "I can be president of the United States or I can control Alice. I cannot possibly do both."

And if you want to find out how another president coped with two of the biggest, meanest, toughest challenges ever, just go ahead and turn to the very next page. . . .

Of all the lucky people in America, young Franklin D. Roosevelt was one of the luckiest. He was rich. He was smart. He was popular. And he was determined. Franklin was determined to be like the "greatest man" he knew. He was determined to be just like his cousin Theodore Roosevelt, the president of the United States.

Now, of course, trying to be like a president is usually a very good thing. But Franklin got a little carried away. First, he put on eyeglasses that looked exactly like his cousin Ted's.

Another time, he grew a sort of Ted-mustache.

And since President Theodore liked to say the word, "DEE-lighted," Franklin began to say, "DEE-lighted," too. Still, deep inside, Franklin knew that to truly be like Cousin Ted, he would have to work hard. He would have to work very hard for his country.

So, naturally, he started in.

First, Franklin became a member of the New York Legislature—just like his older cousin Ted. Then Franklin helped to run the US Navy—exactly like his famous cousin Ted. And soon folks began to say that Franklin might become a governor or—even—president. Yes, they said, that youngster Roosevelt is going to do big stuff—exactly like his famous, older cousin, President Ted.

So, of course, you might think that
Franklin's life was just chocolate and sunshine
and roses. And, mostly, it was—until 1921.
Then, soon after his thirty-ninth birthday,
Franklin D. Roosevelt got . . . sick.

One night he felt shivery cold. And two days later Franklin could not stand or move his legs. Doctors said a disease called polio had paralyzed his lower limbs. That meant he would never be able to stand or walk on his own again.

So, there was Franklin: sick and stuck in a wheelchair. Stuck with one great big, gigantic problem. No one knew how to make him well.

But Franklin was determined.

He believed that if you have a problem, solve it. If one solution doesn't work, try another. But, "Above all, TRY SOMETHING."

So, naturally, he did.

To make his body stronger, Franklin exercised. To stand, he stiffened
his limp legs with heavy metal braces. Then he learned to take a few
small steps with crutches. And if people felt sorry for him when he fell,
Franklin just said, "No sob stuff," please. He knew he would get better.

Now, of course, Franklin's family tried to help. When he was too sick
to talk at political meetings, his wife, Eleanor, made speeches for him.
And Franklin's children also helped by cheering for his leg muscles. They
cheered for his thigh muscles and his calf muscles. But they absolutely
"loved" to cheer for his gluteus maximus. That was the extra big muscle
in Franklin's behind.

Slowly, with everyone's help, Franklin got stronger. He got strong enough to lift a 237-pound shark out of the water while he was fishing. He got well enough to drive a specially made car, using only his hands. He even figured out how to stand up on his braced legs long enough to make speeches. Then, because Eleanor made a special effort to introduce Franklin to poor Americans and working Americans, he learned a lot about how ordinary US citizens lived. And when friends asked if he could take a big step and run for the job of governor of New York, Franklin said: Yes. I can.

Now, no disabled person had ever tried to become a governor, a president, or even a mayor before, so, of course, some people objected. They said that a handicapped person like Franklin was not strong enough to carry out the business of government. But Franklin's friends just answered, PHOOEY! A governor's business "is brain work," they said. "The governor of New York State does not have to be an acrobat." And that made sense. It made such good sense that New Yorkers elected Franklin D. Roosevelt.

So, of course, you might think that life was just chocolate and sunshine and roses. And in some ways it was . . . until 1929. Then, while Franklin was trying to do good work as governor, America got . . . sick.

Some people thought this business sickness (which historians call the Great Depression) started with one event. And some people said it started with another. But everybody knew that in 1929 a whole lot of well-off people suddenly went broke because they lost all their money gambling on the New York City stock market. Then a lot of farmers and workers went broke. They went broke because no one would pay enough for their crops and services. Soon many factories and stores fired all their employees and shut down because most folks couldn't afford to buy their products.

And when out-of-work people tried to withdraw their money, thousands of banks went broke, closed their doors, and went completely out of business. Millions of people lost their jobs, and soon one out of every four American grown-ups had no work. Many lived in cardboard shacks because they couldn't afford to pay the rent. Some looked in garbage cans for food. Others stood in line to get a piece of bread.

Everything was going wrong. And everyone was very, very scared.

So, there was America: sick and broke and scared and stuck. Stuck with one great big, gigantic problem. In Washington, US government officials shook their heads. They said they couldn't fix the mess.

But Franklin was determined. He believed that if you have a problem, solve it. If one solution doesn't work, try another. But "Above all, TRY SOMETHING."

And he decided to run for president.

Now, of course, some people objected. They said that a paralyzed man was not strong enough to lead a troubled nation.

But Franklin told voters: I can do it. I can solve this country's problems.

And Americans listened. Hmmm, they said. If this Roosevelt guy can beat polio, he can probably beat anything. So in 1932 they elected him president.

But solving the problems of a whole country was one mighty big job. And, sometimes, even Franklin D. Roosevelt wondered if he could really do it. So, at a church service before he was sworn in as president, Franklin knelt for a long time, holding his head in his hands—probably hoping for strength.

Then he got up and got started.

First, at the inauguration—or presidential swearing-in ceremony—Franklin did not sit in his wheelchair. He stood up. With his braces, a cane, and the help of his son, Franklin stood up on his paralyzed legs and Americans saw that both sick people and sick nations could get better.

Then, as the whole nation listened, Franklin Roosevelt told people not to be afraid. Fear, he said, just makes folks give up and stop trying.

And that, Franklin told Americans, is why: "The only thing we have to fear is fear itself."

Besides, Franklin said, I am determined. I am determined to "act and act quickly" to solve this nation's problems.

So, naturally, he did.

He put the government to work so fast that after the inauguration lights stayed on practically all night in official buildings all over Washington.

Then, because people had no money, Franklin had Congress pass a new law that put banks back in business.

But, of course, what America really needed was jobs. So Franklin tried another new thing. He had the government put Americans to work. He gave some Americans jobs building dams, highways, tunnels . . .

... parks, schools, and bridges. He gave artists jobs painting pictures and shoemakers jobs making shoes. Once there was even a government circus that hired out-of-work clowns and acrobats.

TIME WOUNDS ALL HEELS.

THE STUPENDOUS CIRCUS

CLOWNS GALORE!

But that still didn't solve all the nation's problems. So, Franklin found new ways to help farmers. For the first time he had the government give pensions to old people and money to people who had lost their jobs.

But was all this new stuff helping? Was it fixing America? Franklin had to know.

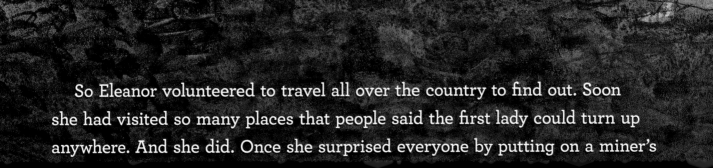

So Eleanor volunteered to travel all over the country to find out. Soon she had visited so many places that people said the first lady could turn up anywhere. And she did. Once she surprised everyone by putting on a miner's

But even Eleanor couldn't find out everything, so Franklin talked to Americans on the radio. "My friends," he said, "I want to know, are you better off?"

And people answered. Eight thousand letters a day poured into the White House.

And some of those letters said, YES, "I feel 100% better."

But other letters said, NO, ". . . I am not better." And lots of folks just grumbled. Some said that Franklin was doing too much, spending too much government money, and ruining the country. They called him "Rattlesnake Roosevelt." And some soreheads just wanted Franklin to shut up. "Please stop talking, and get off the radio," they said. "We want to hear some music."

But, even while those soreheads were grumbling, America was getting a little better. First, a few factories and stores reopened. Then, a few unemployed men and women found jobs. And when Franklin visited Chicago, thousands paraded down the streets with him.

People pointed and yelled out, "He saved my home."
"He gave me a job."

So, naturally, when Franklin ran for president again
in 1936, even more people voted for him.

And on Inauguration Day, when Franklin stood on his braced legs to be sworn in again as president, people cheered.

They cheered because, even though he couldn't walk, Franklin D. Roosevelt had taken big steps. He had taken big steps to help America.

SEE THE BRAND NEW COUNTRY!

The Washington Post

ROOSEVELT SWORN IN TODAY

PROMISES QUICK ACTION TO CONGRESS

WILL SPEAK TO THE NATION

I Want ROOSEVELT Again

CARRY ON ROOSEVELT

ROOSEVELT

FDR

FDR

FDR

ROOSEVELT

BEGINS TERM

WARTIME PRESIDENT